CLEANING TIPS FOR FREE SPIRITS AND OTHER SLOBS, INCLUDING MEN AND THE FEEBLE

BY

MARTHA WALDEN

Cover design by Annie Reid
Interior art by Yavanna Reynolds

Thank you, Sally Cairnes Wuster, Dyani Walden, and Elaine Weinreb for proofreading and advice.

ISBN-13: 978-1481050265

Introduction

People pay me to clean their houses. They're too busy to do it themselves—too busy working, too busy with other activities. Or maybe they just plain hate to clean. I don't care. Their priorities have my blessings. I'm not exactly laughing all the way to the bank, but I'm smiling! I charge a good wage for what I do.

You could probably use some help yourself. Like my clients, you have more shall-we-say creative uses for your limited time. Can't afford someone like me? Oh, that's too bad.

Luckily, there is no law that says you have to keep your house tidy. It's a free country, right? A clean house is just a matter of aesthetics. As long as you're not contaminating yourself and your loved ones, of course. As long as you're not tripping over stuff all the time, and you can find what you need, and you're not particularly sensitive to dust and pet hair, you're fine!

But we're on a slippery slope here. A mess can go over the line really fast and repel even a hardcore free spirit like yourself. One day you pick up a book or something that is so filthy your first instinct is to drop it and run. My God, you think, where did this come from?

But you can see where it came from—right there on the shelf in front of you, and everything else on that shelf is also covered with cobwebs and dirt. You look around you, amazed. You're seeing things you've never quite seen before, and it shakes you up a little.

When you can't put off cleaning any longer, this book is your best bet. You want a pragmatic expert like me on your side, someone who's familiar with the term, "good enough." I answer the questions you've been afraid to ask. I identify the corners you can cut, and tell you when you're better off just buckling down.

In addition to the most useful tools and cleaning substances, I describe the easiest and most effective cleaning techniques. When it's time to clean, you don't want to mess around.

When I say *easy,* I'm serious. I've developed techniques that are specifically about reducing the physical strain of cleaning. I even have some advice about the psychological strain.

I got my housecleaning badge the hard way. For most of my adult life, I was a head-in-the-clouds type who seldom even noticed my immediate surroundings. Living in a dirty house was not a problem for me. But when I was forty-five years old I lost a job at the worst possible time. Financial crisis had me in its claws almost immediately. In sheer desperation I put out signs on bulletin boards, advertising my services as a housecleaner. How hard could it be?

Talk about a crash course! I didn't do a very good job at first. Who knew that dust collected on lampshades? For years it never occurred to me to lift up the edge of rugs, and it was a shock when I finally did. How about that little patch of wilderness between the toilet and the wall? It's a regular ecosystem if you let it go long enough.

But I learned. After a while, I started taking satisfaction in my newfound ability to notice dirt and clutter and to do something about it. Now I'm like Dr. Jekyll and Mr. Hyde.

On the job, I pounce on the slightest dust, but at home . . . Well, let's just say a clean house still isn't my number one priority. The hours are short, and I do my best to enjoy them.

But when it's time to clean I know exactly what to do and how to go about it in the most efficient and effective way possible.

If I can do it you can too! And that goes for you men out there. I used to hate cleaning as much as any man alive. I do not believe that women have an innate ability for it. If you're a guy who shares a house or apartment with a woman, don't stick her with all the cleaning.

No whining either. And that goes for everybody.

Section One – Equip Yourself

Section Two – Time to Clean

EQUIP YOURSELF

When I first started cleaning houses for a living, I rode a bike to my clients' houses and used whatever tools and cleaning products they had available. But as the years went by, I formed distinct preferences. Now I drive a truck to work, and it is stocked. So much for the lean, mean, green approach to business.

I shall now tell you exactly what you need. The right tool for the job will boost not only your effectiveness but also your morale. The same goes for substances (for the house, not you!). So many cleaning products on the shelves are expensive and completely unnecessary. Find out what you really need before you go to the store.

Chapter one

TOOLS THAT WORK

The right tool makes the job easier and faster. But all the right tools in the world aren't going to help you if you can't find them. So keep your cleaning tools together and accessible. The more time and energy it takes to find the right tool, the less time and energy you have for using it. If you have to turn the garage upside down to find the bucket, you're probably not going to mop the kitchen floor today.

Broom

Synthetic bristles are more thorough than straw. Whether straw or synthetic, the broom will last longer if you don't store it standing on its bristles. Either hang it from a hook or stand it upside down.

Brushes

Hard-bristled

Scrub brushes are a good example of a hard-bristled brush. They're a big help when it comes to loosening and cleaning off thick, chunky crud or objects that have a lot of ridges and texture. [See chapter 9 for technique tips.]

Grout brush

It's the size of a toothbrush with hard fiberglass bristles. I found mine at a hardware store. But don't worry if you can't find one. I used to live without one, so I guess you can too. A toothbrush works.

Soft-bristled

Toothbrushes and back-scrubbers have soft bristles that work well on finished wood and drywall and finely textured surfaces.

Soft, longer bristles can be good for dusting. [See illustration on pg. 4.]

Bucket

The best bucket for cleaning—especially mopping floors--is divided into two compartments: one side for soapy water, one for rinse water. But if you can't find this type of bucket at the hardware store, you can improvise. [See mopping floors in chapter 8.]

Dusters

Dusters distinguish practical cleaners, who have a life, from purists who go around checking furniture with a white-gloved finger. I use a duster on just about everything, and if I have the time, I'll come back with a cloth to wipe the most prominent and accessible surfaces—like the coffee table, for instance. This two-phased approach is actually better for the furniture than applying furniture polish to a very dusty surface. You don't want to swap dust for grime.

The trick with dusters is to clean them frequently—a few seconds is all it takes—and to use the right technique. [See chapter 7.]

Overhead duster with extension stick

Even the white-gloved people will use an overhead duster—a globular brush on an extension stick—to deal with cobwebs and dusty surfaces that are too high to reach without a ladder.

The type that is common in department stores and hardware stores has a telescoping handle of about six feet. Added to the height of the user, it reaches most ceilings. If you have high ceilings, you should get a longer extension stick.

Feather duster

A feather duster will save you a lot of time and effort. In addition to furniture, you can use it on the tops of books, light bulbs and the insides of lampshades, door frames, the tops of light fixtures, plant leaves, knickknacks, fragile things and other stuff too maddening to wipe with a cloth.

Tools that Work

Lamb's wool duster

This is basically a wad of wool—about a foot long and three inches in diameter--on a stick. The lanolin of the wool attracts dust, so less dust goes into the air than when you use a feather duster. However, they're clumsier than feather dusters when it comes to cluttered surfaces or reaching up inside a lampshade, for instance.

I use my lamb's wool duster to reach under furniture or for those inconvenient small spaces that occur between bookshelves and a wall, for instance, or under the couch. You can improvise with a rag wrapped around a stick.

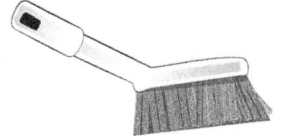

Dusting Brush

Sometimes you need to get in there with something a little stiffer and more pointed than either feathers or lamb's wool. Try a whiskbroom with soft bristles about two or three inches long. I use it to dust a real variety of things—blinds that are starting to get a little grimy, slanted slats like you find on closet doors or furnace radiators, furniture with ledges and carvings, in between the spokes or slats of chairs It also comes in handy for anything rough-textured—like bricks and hearth stones and rough-hewn wooden mantles.

Latex or plastic gloves

You want to protect your hands for some jobs, and I leave it to you to decide which ones. Unless you work in a hospital, re-usable gloves should suffice. But be prepared to forfeit the use of your fingernails.

Buy ones that are big enough to take on and off easily. Cleaning can be annoying enough without peeling wet latex off your hands, digit by digit.

Mop

Sponge mops and string mops seem equally effective to me, but sponge mops are lighter than string mops and easier to wring out. Plus it's easier with sponge mops to vary the amount of water you want to apply to the floor.

However, the sponges get grungy and start disintegrating fairly soon. You can slow this process down by giving the mop an extra good rinse and wring when you finish the job. Then hang the mop up somewhere so air can get to it. Do <u>not</u> stand it upside down.

Stock up on the replacement sponges, so you'll have one when you need it. Otherwise, you'll end up buying a whole new mop when you can't find the right replacement sponge. This bothers me more than it does the mop manufacturers.

Putty knife

I use a putty knife, wrapped with a few rag layers, for cleaning the edge of a floor or counter, or the tops of baseboards, or any narrow space—like behind water fixtures. It's not only more effective but easier on your muscles, joints, and tendons. [See scrubbing techniques in chapter 9.]

Quart-sized plastic containers

Yogurt containers are perfect. I use one filled with hot soapy water for cleaning counters, etc. I use two of them for filling my mop bucket from a kitchen or bathroom sink. One sits under the faucet and fills up while I empty the other one into the bucket. This same basic technique works also for rinsing out bathtubs and sinks that don't have a pullout spray nozzle.

Rags

Rags are superior in every way to sponges. More effective, more versatile, more sanitary, more environmental. And they're free if you tear up old towels, etc. People used rags for cleaning long before sponges wormed their way into the modern household.

I often find sponges sitting next to my clients' sinks that are so disgusting that I just throw them away. I can't restrain myself. [For more about the gross qualities of sponges, see chapter 5.]

Rags can be laundered and used over and over. They can be sized and shaped depending on the job. In general, smaller sizes are better than big wads of fabric. See the sidebar on next page for more information about specific fabrics.

Squeegee

You'll never catch me attacking windows with paper towel and Windex like an amateur. Or newspaper and vinegar. I never cleaned a window to my satisfaction in my whole life until I learned how to wield a squeegee. Unless you have lots of large windows, a twelve-inch squeegee is probably the most useful size. [See windows in chapter 8.]

Swiffer or dust mop

The rectangular flat surface of a Swiffer is designed for attaching the manufacturer's own disposable "cloths" of both a wet or dry variety. I avoid disposable stuff like that, so I attach a rag, sprayed with vinegar or Bona. [See floor cleaners in chapter 3.] This arrangement is good for dusting and cleaning mildly dirty wooden floors without using water.

The tool lays flat, so you can dust or damp-mop under couches and other low furniture. It also swivels, so you can move forward in side-to-side motions without having to lift it up from the floor.

I prefer the Swiffer to the old-fashioned dust mop because it's easier to launder the rags than to un-attach, launder, and re-attach the dust mop head.

Vacuum

The boss tool gets its very own chapter.

RAG CONNOISSEUR GUIDE

Rags have three functions—scrubbing, absorbing, and polishing.

Cotton knits -- best for polishing furniture and cleaning glass
Cotton weaves (tight) – very good at polishing and absorbing, okay at scrubbing
Denim -- fairly good at absorbing and polishing
Diapers -- super at absorbing and good at polishing
Flannel – excellent dust rag if it's not linty
Synthetic / cotton blends -- pretty good at polishing
Terry cloth -- great for scrubbing and absorbing but not much good at polishing

---

Your own notes

Chapter two

WELCOME TO THE MACHINE

If you want to go back to the good old days before electricity and vacuum cleaners, try sweeping a rug. You can do it— particularly a low-pile one—but you raise a lot of dust in the process. That's why the old cleaning manuals recommended cleaning the floor before dusting the furniture. Back when I lived off the grid, I used to tie a rag around my nose when I swept the rug.

You can make a pretty good case for using a broom on hard-surface floors. People have attached a little shock of straw to a stick and used it to sweep the floor for millennia. So it doesn't get every little particle up off the floor. How pristine does a floor need to be? We walk on it, right? However, they say the finish on a hardwood floor wears out more quickly when you're crunching those little particles underfoot.

I usually sweep hard-surface floors at home, but I have to admit that I prefer the electrical power of a vacuum for all floors when I'm on the job. It removes dust and dirt thoroughly and instantly, and the crevice tool pokes back into tight corners and under things. Plus, the mechanical power of a vacuum gets my adrenalin moving. I vacuum just about anything that can't run away.

Upright vs. canister

My favorite type of vacuum is the upright with a wand that is already full activated. All you have to do is whip it out like Luke Skywalker. The spiders will run like hell when they see you coming.

The ideal upright has a control that turns off the rug beater but keeps the suction going. Use this setting for floors with no rug. If your vacuum is bottom-of-the-line like mine, it probably doesn't offer that option. So use an attachment for your hard floors; otherwise, the spinning beater will throw a lot of the dirt to the side, and you'll keep recognizing the same crud as you vacuum it up over and over.

Also, the beater bar is not recommended for use on hardwood floors. It's supposed to be too rough.

People with really bad backs may do better with a canister-style vacuum because you don't have to push it. On the other hand you have to drag it along behind you like a reluctant dog you're trying to walk, and it's always getting hung up on the furniture.

However, canister vacuums usually have a larger and better attachment for hard floors than uprights do.

Please spare me your antique Kirby. Yes, it's a marvel that the thing is still running in this day and age, and yes, it still cleans the bejesus out of any rug. But it's heavy. Plus you have to unbolt the entire rug beater in order to replace it with the attachment hose, which makes it even more awkward to drag around. Your great-grandma was doubtlessly thrilled when her husband broke down and endowed her with one, but she was made of sterner stuff than me.

Bagged vs. bagless

There are two kinds of people in this world— those who are appalled by the messiness of emptying a dirt cup into the trash (the cloud of dust! the filth that hangs up inside sometimes! the necessity of washing your hands afterwards!); and those who just take the thing outside to the trash bin and empty it.

The bag people say it's much more convenient to toss a bag

How effective is your vacuum technique?

Do you dart all over the room like you're trying to win a marathon? Do you vacuum up objects before you have a chance to identify them? Do you go over the same swath of carpet three or four times before it looks clean?

Do you keep the vacuum adjusted to its lowest height? That's what I used to do. I thought the harder the vacuum was to push, the more powerful its suction was.

Wrong! The suction is more powerful when there is a little space between the vacuum and the rug. Set it high enough to reduce the resistance, and slow down for pity's sake. Vacuuming is not an Olympic event.

---

into the indoor trash than to trek outside with the dust container. That might seem true, especially if it's raining or snowing outside, but think of what is not being counted here. How convenient is it to have to stock the right bags for your particular model?

This inconvenience begins with trying to find the right type of bag (now what is the model name and number of your vacuum again?) and extends through keeping them somewhere in the closet where you can find them.

The question of what is better—bagged or bagless—may be answered by your sensitivity to dust. The bagged ones are supposed to have better filtration systems. Plus, with some models, you can actually choose which level of filtration you want. If you're asthmatic or have allergies, you want HEPA (high efficiency particulate air) bags.

I myself have never noticed a dust problem with bagless vacuums, but if I were particularly sensitive to dust I probably wouldn't be cleaning houses for a living.

Bags are not infallible. They break or otherwise come unsealed, and the kicker is that you don't know it's happened until the situation is far advanced.

Bags also fill up, and you don't realize it until the motor has lost some of its horsepower. With a bagless model you can see exactly what is going on.

Just in case you're in the market for a vacuum cleaner, and you decide to buy a bagless model, make sure you get one with filters that you can clean yourself instead of ones you have to replace.

Troubleshooting vacuums

12

Welcome to the Machine

The most common problem with a vacuum is easy to fix. I keep a long skinny rod in my truck box for unplugging the hose. You can usually tell when a vacuum plugs up because the tone of the motor changes. But sometimes your first clue is its loss of power.

If you're uncertain you have full suction power or not, try to vacuum up a quarter. You should be able to hear it clank if it makes it to the bag or canister.

If the vacuum starts making a high-pitched, outraged sound, and you smell something burning, turn it off quick! You might save the belt from breaking. Let it cool down a few minutes before you turn it back on and check to see if the rug beater is still twirling. If it isn't, you were too late to save the belt.

The most frequent cause of a belt breaking is the vacuum catching hold of something that is way too big—like fringes of a rug or the edge of a bedspread. But sometimes it breaks just because it's old. You may have to take it to the repair shop if you're not strong enough to replace the belt yourself.

The worst thing about vacuums is that they're loud. But they're not so loud that audiologists recommend ear protection while using them. However, it's hard to listen to music when you're vacuuming. That right there is a good reason to take a break from the machine once in a while. Get out the good old quiet broom. You don't even have to plug it in.

Your own notes

Chapter three

THE RIGHT STUFF

I favor natural substances over products with a lot of dubious chemicals in them. Some of those products have very specific uses that may not apply anymore, so you end up with a shelf full of unneeded toxic compounds. But you're afraid to throw them in the trash because they're probably hazardous to the environment.

You don't have that problem with rubbing alcohol and baking soda, for instance. You use them for many different things, and they're safe to store. They're better than detergents and other chemicals for the environment, especially rivers. They're also pretty cheap—always a plus in my book.

Some cleaning products aren't so healthy for our personal exposure either. Oven cleaner, for instance, makes my scalp twitch just looking at the can. Other chemicals are also hard on the skin and can affect the liver.

However, I am not a purist. My policy is to use non-toxic, completely safe substances whenever feasible, but I just don't worry about it when I need a little bleach or a petro-chemical once in a while. Sometimes you gotta roll out the big guns.

Baking soda

You can make pancakes with it and then use it to clean the stove. Use baking soda on enameled metals—like stovetops-- and stainless steel, ceramics, and plastics. Use it on Formica counters, fiberglass bathtubs, and anything you're frightened to use scouring cleanser on—but NOT on glazed tiles, finished wood or windows. (It won't damage windows, but it streaks like crazy.)

Some cleaning manuals recommend dissolving baking soda in water to make a cleaning solution, but I think that's dumb. Why neutralize its abrasion? I sprinkle baking soda on a damp rag, rub it in a little with my thumb and go for it. (Old parmesan cheese containers make great baking soda dispensers.)

But I have to warn you—there is a disadvantage to using baking soda. It is difficult to rinse. If you're not careful, you'll end up with little patches of dried white powder all over the place. I often use my spray bottle of vinegar and water to help rinse it away.

Chlorine Bleach

My favorite bleach cleaner is Soft Scrub. Its thickness

means you can coat vertical and slanting surfaces and let it sit for a while to make the most of its bleaching effect. Add a little baking soda to make a thicker paste, and it will stretch farther too.

It's cheaper, of course, to simply mix bleach and water—one ounce in a pint of water should do the trick—but it doesn't stick to slanting surfaces.

Use bleach as a disinfectant. See sidebar on the next page for more information about disinfectants.

To be on the safe side, don't mix bleach with anything other than water or detergents. It's too easy to manufacture your very own toxic gas

Bleach Warning

Bleach can cause serious environmental problems when used on an industrial scale. Household use isn't that bad, particularly since wastewater treatment plants remove the stuff. I figure the less they have to deal with, the better. That's why I minimize my use of bleach.

Also, bleach is not good for the respiratory system, especially the lungs. Bear in mind that it was the first chemical weapon. It made its debut in WWI. So don't go hog-wild with the stuff, and open a window.

De-Solv-it

It's an orange-based concoction that is much more effective than Citra-Solv. I use it against glue and other adhesives, like the type used with labels, plus silicone, paint, and tar, tree sap, candle wax, and grass stains.

Elbow Grease

Use this stuff in small quantities. Don't throw it around. Enhance its effectiveness with good technique. Brute force is not always the best approach even if you're young. [See chapter 9 for tips on reducing the strain.]

Floor cleaners

Disinfectants

Two teaspoons of bleach to a quart of water is your best bet for disinfecting (ten minutes of constant contact) or sanitizing (thirty to sixty seconds). Other common household substances have anti-microbial properties—like vinegar, hydrogen peroxide, and rubbing alcohol. But they're less versatile than bleach. Vinegar, for instance, works great against salmonella but not e coli. Also, I can't find reliable information about contact time when using these other substances.

Since we can't do a poll to find out what germs are present, it makes sense to use something that will kill most of them. So if you're going to go to the trouble of killing germs, do it as reliably as possible with bleach. [See chapter 5 for more about disinfecting and sanitizing.]

Bona

This spray-on cleaner is supposed to be environmentally friendly, but these days depleted uranium says Green! on the label. GoodGuide gives it a 5.4, which is a tiny bit above average.

It's especially formulated for damp mopping of wooden and laminate floors. You don't have to dry the floor.

Oil soaps

Murphy's and Eco-ver are my two favorite oil soaps. An oil soap is made from oil—like linseed oil—which is what everyone used before detergents were invented.

The reason everyone switched to detergents is that many people back then used hard water, which often caused a scum to form when combined with soap—a real problem for laundry in particular. All things considered, there is no reason to not use soap on the floor.

I use oil soaps on both wooden and non-wooden floors. If the floor is really dirty, I increase the proportion of soap to water [See mopping floors in chapter 8.]

Spic n' Span

On the other hand, I am not one hundred percent opposed to

breaking out the hard stuff on non-wooden floors. Some
floors just cry out for it. You'll recognize them when you see
them.

Furniture Polish

Furniture polish is not really necessary unless you've just
used a cleaning agent that dries wood. I've gone for a long
time without using any polish, and the furniture seems fine.
But I eventually can't resist putting some on a rag and
massaging the furniture with it. I think it's the smell. It's an
olfactory reward for cleaning the house.

New Age Household Cleaner

This is a very effective, mostly natural detergent. It
biodegrades in fourteen to twenty-four hours. I use it for
everything from walls and windows to floors. It cleans walls
as effectively as TSP. It probably doesn't rinse as thoroughly,
however. That's why painters recommend TSP for preparing
walls for painting.

Pumice stick

You buy this stuff at hardware stores. It really is a volcanic
rock. It cleans some things that nothing else works on. For
instance, enameled sinks often form little rings around the
drain that respond only to pumice. Carbon build-ups on
enameled teakettles and the inside of ovens come right off
with the pumice treatment.

But use it sparingly and only as a last resort. Something that
strong probably wears down porcelain and other finishes in
the long run.
Pumice is safest when you scrape the stick with a putty knife
to make a fine grit. Then squirt a little detergent on the spot

you're cleaning to act as a lubricant for the pumice grit. Scrub with a rag.

Choose your level of abrasion

Baking soda is the safest form of abrasion. Try it first.

Bon Ami is a little more effective than baking soda, but it's not as safe. I use it occasionally on fiberglass and acrylic tubs, etc. without apparent damage, but it may eventually take a toll.

Other scouring cleansers—Comet, Ajax--are a little more abrasive than Bon Ami, more apt to damage finishes over time, plus many of them contain bleach these days. Good? Bad? I guess it depends. I'll add my own bleach if it's necessary, thank you very much.

Steel Wool has the reputation of being very abrasive, but the finest grade (0000) can be used on windows.

Pumice is the heavyweight champion that doesn't take no for an answer. But you have to be careful with it. See previous page for instructions.

When using any abrasive, spread out the pressure so you're not bearing down really hard on one small spot.

If you use the stick directly, lay it flat on its side to reduce the danger of scratching.

When I'm cleaning porcelain and stove enamels, I use it on thick build-ups, but when I get close to the finish, I switch to really fine steel wool See sidebar this page.

Rubbing alcohol

Rubbing alcohol is what I call a "dab cleaner." You put just a little on a rag and use it on things that you don't want to get wet—like the keyboard of a computer or other electronic components. It's particularly good at removing fingertip smudges.

I took honey off the cover of a magazine once with rubbing alcohol. You couldn't tell that anything had happened to it.

Or remove spots from a mirror when you don't want to wash the whole thing. It smears a little bit, so use the dry end of your cloth to polish.

Don't use rubbing alcohol on furniture—some finishes react badly.

Scouring powder

I am a big fan of mild abrasion. It's a cheap, effective way to scrub hard surfaces such as stainless steel sinks and unglazed tiles, linoleum, glass shower doors, toilets and other porcelain surfaces.

However, scouring powder may gradually erode porcelain finishes. Some professional cleaners advise against any kind of abrasion when cleaning. I compromise and use Bon Ami, the least abrasive of the scouring powders. It's still a big help. It costs a little more than Comet or Ajax, but it's still one of the cheapest cleaning agents you will find on the market. Buy it at a hardware store.

I occasionally use Bon Ami on both acrylic and fiberglass tubs and shower stalls without apparent damage. But the experts advise against using anything abrasive on acrylic and fiberglass.

Steel wool

When you buy steel wool at the hardware store, make sure you buy the package with the most zeroes on it. You want the finest grade they make or else risk scratching things. 0000 steel wool will clean windows, enameled metals, and stainless steel—like teakettles.

White vinegar

I've trained my clients to associate the faint aroma of vinegar with a clean house. I keep about a fifty/fifty solution of vinegar and water in a spray bottle that is never far from my reach. Because I have it so ready, I often use it as a first strike on anything that provokes me. Sometimes all you need is something wet. If it fails I try something else.

Vinegar is effective against soap scum, mildew, mold and some hard water and calcium deposits. Use it on glass, stainless steel, brass, bronze, and copper fixtures.

I've read that vinegar can damage ceramic tiles, but my 50/50 solution has never hurt tiles. I've also read in various cleaning manuals that vinegar cuts grease, but I don't think it's true. If you want to cut grease, use baking soda or detergent.

Mostly, I use my vinegar and water combo as a rinse and final wipe on counters and other surfaces after cleaning them with detergent or baking soda. It deodorizes and even has some anti-microbial properties, although it is not recommended as a disinfectant. See sidebar on page 18 for information about disinfectants.

Your own notes

You've assembled your tools—that was probably good for a couple of weeks' delay. Now it's

TIME TO CLEAN

When I started cleaning houses for a living the first thing I had to change was my attitude. Surliness was not useful, especially with my mother absent. Pure self-preservation drove me to find ways to make the experience more pleasant. Here are some pointers for your resistant psyche.

Put on some music! Music helps your body stay relaxed yet energized. If there is no music when it's time to clean, I sing. If I have to suffer, everyone else should too.

Don't hurry. Hurrying strains your body and guarantees you won't get any pleasure out of your work. And you probably won't save significant time either. Organizing and thinking about what you're doing will save much more time than rushing around.

Clean room-by-room rather than doing all the dusting or vacuuming or mopping in the whole house all at once. Room by room grants you some variety of motions. That means less monotony, plus each time you finish a room, you feel like you're making progress. Also, it's easier on your body.

Introducing the 90% rule! It takes more energy and patience to nab the last 10% of dust and dirt than the first 90%. So don't be a perfectionist! No one notices anyway, and it's just going to get dirty again.

Pay attention to what you're doing. Be curious. If you just go through the motions and expect automatic results, you will burn out sooner. Plus you're more likely to use excessive force when you're acting like a robot.

Speaking of excessive force, that is exactly what you want to avoid even if you're young and still immortal with tendons and joints of well-lubricated steel. Do things the easy way. Consult chapter 9 for techniques that reduce the physical strain of cleaning.

Okay, okay, enough beating around the bush. Now it's

REALLY TIME TO CLEAN

(really)

Chapter four

THE KITCHEN

You can only eat take-out for so long

If you have only five minutes to clean, spend them in the kitchen. The kitchen is the heart of the house. If it's clogged with dirty dishes and dirty counters, your whole outlook on life goes downhill. Keep the counters clear as much as possible. If you don't have a dishwasher to stash dirty dishes in, stack them as compactly as you can. Try to keep one sink free.

Refrigerator

How bad is it? Be honest. How long has it been? Is the pickle jar stuck to the shelf? Is gray fuzz creeping out of the vegetable and fruit bins? Has the open box of baking soda run up a white flag?

You should take the shelves and drawers out and wash them in the sink. Yes, it's tempting to think you can clean the shelves where they sit. But you won't really save much time that way, and sticky crud will hide in the crevices. If you resign yourself to your fate right away, it will go pretty fast, and the results are worth it. For the next few days you will be dazzled by the shining white expanses every time you open the refrigerator.

<u>Inside</u>

You can turn the thermostat off first to save electricity, but I have forgotten to turn it back on so many times that I skip that step now.

Unload one shelf onto whatever horizontal surface is closest. Remove the shelf and dunk it into hot sudsy water in the sink. Then pull up a small table or even a chair to use for the contents of the next shelf. When you've unloaded the second shelf, wash and dry the first shelf while the second one is soaking. Put it back and replace the food. Then go for the third one.

You get the idea, right? When you do it shelf by shelf, you minimize the amount of time that food sits outside the refrigerator. Plus it's easier to put things back the way they were.

Stubborn stuff on the sides of the refrigerator responds to baking soda. Sprinkle a little directly on your wet rag, rub it in, and scrub. Use a dryer rag to wipe off the residue.

<u>Outside</u>

Baking soda also works really well—better than soap--on the outside of a refrigerator. It gets into all the little cracks of textured plastic. Rinse with vinegar and water and wipe dry. If your refrigerator is stainless steel, refer to instructions for stainless steel counters in the sidebar on pg. 30.

<u>Freezer</u>

Whether a compartment of your refrigerator or a stand-alone, the freezer doesn't typically require much attention. Use a little rubbing alcohol on a rag to clean small smears from the sides or bottom. Alcohol has a lower freezing point than water, so it works better under freezing conditions.

Ice may eventually form on the sides. Don't let it get too thick if it does. Put the contents into a cooler or a box lined with towels, and turn the control to off to allow the ice to melt. (Don't forget to turn it back on.) Fling hot water on it to hurry it up.

Refrigerator maintenance

Once in a while—let's say annually—you should clean off the condenser coils. You just might prolong the life of your refrigerator.

If your refrigerator is air-cooled, the coils are the looped wire things on the back of the refrigerator. You might have to pull the refrigerator away from the wall to reach them with a brush or a vacuum attachment.

If your refrigerator is fan-cooled, the coils are underneath, behind the toe grille. While you're under there, check to see if you have little drain pans with nasty-looking liquid in them. If so, I would empty them if I were you.

Stove

A greasy, cruddy stove is God's punishment for cooking. The more wonderful and elaborate the meal, the worse the stove looks afterwards. When you can't use it without setting off the smoke alarm, you'll know you've let it go too long. Clean it or evacuate!

Ceramic

This is the easiest. Nothing to take apart or clean under—just a level glassy top. Make sure you wait until it has cooled before you clean it. Restrain yourself. Just use soap and water if there is no crusty build up. If there is, baking soda will take care of that, but you have to rinse it extra well—vinegar and water helps--because the tiniest residue will crystallize the next time you fire the stove back up.

Regular gas and electric ranges

If it's really greasy and crusty, take all the removable parts off—grates, pans, knobs—and toss them in a sink full of hot suds. Let them soak for as long as you like, but two weeks is probably not necessary.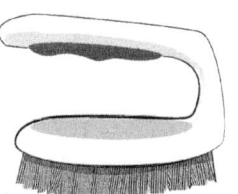

Use baking soda or Bon Ami when it's time to scour. If you're dealing with something really stubborn, use pumice—but only on parts of the stove that are enameled. [See instructions for using pumice in chapter 3.]

But wait a minute before attacking the stove pans. I've seen pans that were totally black with a hard baked-on carbon coating. If yours have reached that level of . . . let's call it seasoning, you may want to think twice before you challenge the status quo. Maybe spontaneous black isn't such a bad color. Just give them a quick once-over with a scrub brush to get the easy stuff off.

If the knobs still look bad after soaking, put them back on the stove to hold them in place and scrub with a toothbrush.

Electric burner coils

Scrape off anything caked on so it won't smoke the next time you turn the stove on. If the offending piece of crud is plastic, you can try using a hairdryer to soften it up enough to scrape.

The Mysterious Netherworld of the Stove

The entire tops of many stoves are hinged and will lift up to expose the place where the grossest gunk accumulates. Every once in a great while, prop it open. Use a putty knife and the crevice tool of your vacuum to get the worst of it out. Go for eighty-five to ninety per cent. Coast on your reputation for a few years.

Ovens

Touchy counters

Marble
Never use vinegar. Immediately wipe up wine, fruit juice and other acids. No abrasive or caustic cleaners should be used, or polish or waxes.

Butcher Block
Despite its appearance and name, butcher block is not a built-in cutting board. It stains very easily. Don't cut up any food directly on it unless you don't mind having a visual record of past menus. Clean it with baking soda or liquid detergent and a scrub brush. Oil it once a year with mineral or tung oil.

Stainless Steel
Don't use anything abrasive, not even baking soda. You're not supposed to use Windex either, but that seems to work pretty well. Whether you use Windex or liquid detergent, rinsed with vinegar and water, a quick buff afterwards with a dry cloth makes it shine.

Glazed Tiles
Don't use anything abrasive, not even baking soda. It will dull the finish. Vinegar and water should be fine as long as it's no stronger than a 50/50 mix.

If you don't have a self-cleaning oven, consider getting one! Cleaning the oven is the nastiest job in the whole house. If you're cavalier about toxic chemicals, go ahead and use commercial oven cleaner, but don't invite me over while you're doing it.

Here's how to clean a really gunked-up oven without the oven cleaner. Put a layer of baking soda or Bon Ami over the baked-on parts, then lay a sopping, hot, soapy rag on top and let sit for at least fifteen minutes.

When you're finished with the soaking, scrape off as much as comes easily with a putty knife sheathed with a rag. Careful use of pumice comes next. [See chapter 3 for instructions under pumice.] If you're worried about scratching the finish, switch to fine steel wool (0000) to get the last of the carbon off.

<u>Range Hood</u>

Clean it with baking soda and rinse with vinegar and water. I advise doing this before you clean the stove underneath it. If you have a removable screen up in there, run it through the dishwasher once in a while.

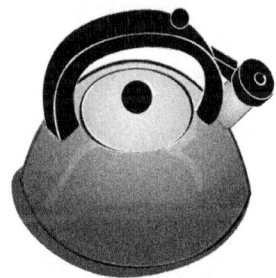

Tea Kettle

When the kettle gets really groady—baked on grease and carbon—you need special measures. I recommend pumice for enameled kettles. You'll be amazed at how easily that stuff comes off. (At least I am—but maybe I have a low amazement threshold.)

Blackened stainless steel kettles require fine steel wool. Don't press very hard—just patiently rub it back and forth.

Counters

Laminated, tiled, and granite counters are cleaned in pretty much the same way. See sidebar entitled "Touchy Counters" for exceptions to the rule.

I like to fill a quart-sized container with liquid detergent and water, so I don't have to keep running the water. Instead of using a groady sponge that has been breeding by the side of the sink, use a dishrag to clean the counters. It's not only more sanitary, it's more effective.

A dishrag lets you feel the counter through the cloth if you spread it out a little. Expend your energy where it's needed and just wipe the rest. For really crusty areas slop on soap and water and come back in a few minutes to finish the job.

I squirt the counters with vinegar and water to rinse them, particularly if I've used a lot of soapy water. A wipe with a more or less dry towel is the finishing touch. This final wipe, by the way, prevents smearing. It separates the pros from the amateurs.

Every once in a while, a deeper cleaning is called for. For those occasions refer to the sidebar on this page.

Stains

Stains on laminate and unglazed tile counters often respond to baking soda. Use it like scouring powder. Glazed tiles, however, might be too touchy for any abrasive, even baking soda. [See sidebar on pg. 30.]

Repellant surfaces

Counters and other surfaces can use an occasional deep cleaning because an invisible film of grease forms. You can tell by the way your wash water beads up. Squirt a small amount of detergent directly on your rag and go over the area several times with easy strokes, changing angle slightly each time. See how evenly the suds coat the surface now.

Despite the dire warnings I've read about the "dulling" effect of unrinsed soap, I just squirt the soapy counter with vinegar and water and sop it all up with an absorbent rag. Haven't noticed a problem yet.

A vinegar and water rinse comes in especially handy after using baking soda because vinegar dissolves it.

Soft Scrub also works on stained laminate and tile counters.

<u>Tile grout</u>

The grout between tiles gets pretty grungy, especially in high-use areas. Target those sections with vinegar and water—spray directly onto the grout. Wait a few minutes and then use a toothbrush or a small brush with stiffer bristles. If the vinegar doesn't cut it, dry the counter and start over with bleach and water—about one ounce to a pint—or Soft Scrub.

Dishwasher

They're pretty much self-cleaning and need very little attention. Just clean the seals once in a while with vinegar and water if you see any mildew. If the water ports look gunky, use a pipe cleaner to clear them. If there is a little screen in there, use a stiff brush on it. The outside is cleaned like anything else in the kitchen.

Cabinets and Shelves

If the shelves are unfinished wood, just vacuum them off once in a while if they're accessible. (Use a little whiskbroom if they're too high.) If the shelves are enameled, a damp wipe once in a while will keep them extra nice.

If you're dealing with shelf liner that is old and wrinkled, strip it off (If it won't come off, a hair dryer might heat it up enough to persuade it.) Consider not replacing it.

If the grunge has graduated to gunk (and I'm taking the Fifth about where I've witnessed this), refer to the sidebar on next page.

Enameled cabinet doors

Soap might damage the finish if it's an oil-based paint. Most enamels are probably latex, but when in doubt just use your vinegar and water spray bottle.

Cabinet doors with natural wood finishes

These can be a little more difficult, especially if you've let them go for a long time. You can use a soapy rag wrapped around a scrub brush and the grime will definitely come off. The only problem is that the finish might as well. A gentler approach would be a soft-bristled brush and oil soap. Then rinse and dry.

Really Filthy Shelves

For caked-on, tarry gunk, use really, really hot water, a scrub brush, and a putty knife.

Dribble water directly onto the shelf and distribute it with the scrub brush. After a little light scrubbing and scraping, sop up the muddy water with a rag (which you probably just want to toss afterwards).

Repeat the treatment if necessary. Dry with a towel. Let the wood air-dry a little longer before replacing contents of the shelf. Swear a mighty oath that in the future you will brush and wipe that shelf off before it gets that bad again.

Drawers

Use the crevice tool to vacuum them out.

Microwave

If it's really crusty, microwave a bowl of water for a couple of minutes. That will loosen things up. Wash with soapy water, rinse with vinegar and water. Do a final wipe with a more or less dry rag. Vinegar is a particularly good rinse for the microwave because it deodorizes.

Toaster

Give it a hearty shake and then empty the crumb drawer if it has one. Otherwise, turn it upside down and shake it. No whapping. I used to whap toasters until I whapped one to pieces. Fortunately, it wasn't mine. It belonged to a friend, and now whenever I help her clean the kitchen after having dinner at her house, she eyes her toaster a little anxiously.

Clean the outside of the toaster the same way you clean everything else in the kitchen. Soapy rag, vinegar and water rinse, the final wipe.

If the metal in between the slots has carbon on it, fine steel wool will clean it, but then you really want to shake it well upside down to get rid of steel wool dust. Maybe even stick the crevice tool of the vacuum in there.

Sanitation Issues

Cutting boards, sponges, dish towels, etc. will be discussed in the next chapter, *War on Germs*

Sinks

Stainless steel

> The kitchen is a good place to remember the 90% rule. You can spend a lot of time polishing the stove or the sink, and five minutes later the next meal will instantly wipe out your claim to perfection.

A little Bon Ami goes a long way when you're scrubbing stainless steel sinks. The more you use, the more difficult it is to rinse the sink. Many times I've noticed dried lines of cleanser on the sides of a sink after I thought I'd rinsed it thoroughly.

If you don't have a pullout spray nozzle to use to rinse the sink, use two quart-sized plastic containers. As one fills with water, use the already-filled one to pour water on the sides of the sink.

Porcelain

35

If it's not hopelessly stained, use Bon Ami--or baking soda if you're opposed to using scouring powder on porcelain [See chapter 3 under scouring powder].

Porcelain sinks do tend to get so stained that they're the main exception to my bias against bleach. I like using Soft Scrub because it's thick, so I can coat the entire sink and then let it sit for five minutes or so. I think this method uses less bleach than filling the sink with water and pouring a couple capfuls of straight bleach in.

If you don't have Soft Scrub, sprinkle scouring cleanser as thinly and evenly as you can, then spray it with bleach and water. (one ounce bleach to a pint of water should be strong enough) The scouring cleanser absorbs the bleach and keeps it from simply going down the drain. Let it sit for five minutes or more.

After you've let the mixture sit, use a rag to transfer the bleach-saturated powder to the sides of the sink—a process that will finish off cleaning the bottom of the sink. Let sit some more. Go do something else. Go on. Come back in a few minutes to rinse.

If you're completely opposed to using bleach products, or you just don't have any, sprinkle the bottom of the sink evenly with baking soda and spray heavily with hydrogen peroxide. Let sit for fifteen minutes.

Drains

If your vacuum is handy, use it to suck up the garbage in the basket traps and from the drain itself below the traps. This is much faster and easier than using your fingers or tweezers to fish out little pieces of food. **Caution: you probably shouldn't do this if you just put a fresh bag in your vacuum. It might get wet and tear.**

To give the drain a good scrubbing, coat it with scouring cleanser, stuff a damp scrub rag into the drain—one that is big enough to contact the sides—and rotate it a few times in both directions. Do the same for the basket traps while they're locked into place. Take them out and get most of the slime on the bottom side.

If the drain is plugged up or just really slow, you might be able to clear it out with baking soda and vinegar. See chapter 6 for instructions.

Floor

Are you sure you're finished? Good. See chapter 8 for floor cleaning tips.

Your own notes

Chapter five

WAR ON GERMS

Aaaghhh! They're Coming to Get Us!

On the 1-10 scale of germ vigilance--10 being operating room standards and 1 being blissful oblivion--what number are you? If you're like most people, you probably wander around in the vast in-between. Most of us have no consistent policy. Germs could drive a tank through our bad habits, but once in a while we whip out the Lysol for a good squirt-and-wipe of the usual suspects. Then we award ourselves points for sanitation.

This inconsistent behavior is thoroughly human, but there's a problem with it. Germs are more difficult to kill than what most people think. Those who read the directions on the back of the bottle can see that squirt-and-wipe does not mean a massacre. It probably just kills the old and the unfit and leaves the rest to evolve. If you're going to resort to chemical measures, you should do a thorough job of it.

On the other hand, if you do an effective job and you do it too often, you might be short-changing your immune system. A lot of anecdotal evidence suggests that overly zealous germ-slaying mothers raise kids who develop a lot of allergies. Bacterial, viral, and fungal exposure exercises our immune systems.

Here's my germ policy: I cultivate a few good sanitary habits to avoid breeding germs in my house. Other than that, I don't worry about it unless I have specific reason to go the extra mile and break out the disinfectant. Then I make sure I do a good job. It's not rocket science--just take a few minutes and follow the directions.

If you have an infant or anyone else in your house who might be particularly vulnerable to germs, you should probably read someone else's book.

Sanitary habits in the kitchen

Soap and Water

Use regular liquid detergent and water instead of anti-microbial products to clean your dishes, and regular soap and water for your hands. Washing potential pathogens away is usually effective enough and doesn't encourage them to evolve.

But if you're dealing with raw meat and blood, you should

not only wash your hands immediately afterwards but sanitize or disinfect the affected areas.

Cutting boards and utensils used with raw meat

Don't cut up raw meat on a wooden cutting board or any other cutting board that you are not willing to run through the sanitation cycle of a dishwasher, or immerse in a bleach solution. These are the only two reliable methods for dealing with e coli.

If you're not using a dishwasher with a sanitation cycle, hand wash the cutting board and utensils with soap and water to get rid of all organic matter before immersing them in a chlorine bleach solution for just a few moments. You shouldn't skip the first step. Traces of organic matter can sabotage the disinfecting process.

One teaspoon of bleach per quart of water will kill just about anything you want to kill, plus a lot of innocent microbes who were just minding their own business.

Counters

Don't set backpacks and purses down on counters and tables where food is prepared or eaten. Something nasty could be hitching a ride from wherever you set that pack or purse down in the last few days. The floor of a public bathroom, for instance—or your bathroom, for that matter. Some germs can survive on certain surfaces for several days.

Wash your counters with soap and hot water and a clean dishrag. Sanitize them only when you have reason to believe that they've been contaminated.

Sanitizing the counters takes a little care because you can't immerse them. Wash them in the regular way first to take care of any organic matter. Make your solution of one teaspoon of bleach per quart of water and apply it very liberally with a fresh dishrag. Use enough that it will stay wet for at least thirty seconds. Wipe off the excess and let air-dry.

<u>Sponges</u>

Replace your sponges with dishrags. Sponges are gross. They're magnets for bacterial and fungal growth because they're hard to clean thoroughly, and they take a long time to dry. Most sponges hang out in a damp environment next to the sink—perfect breeding ground.

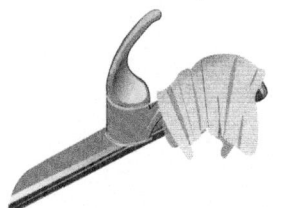 It's much easier to change the dishrag every day than worry about sanitizing the sponge as often as it needs. Some people throw it into the dishwasher, thinking that's a pretty clever trick. But the dishwasher isn't really designed to root food particles out of something porous like a sponge. In fact, it might even insert food particles into the sponge from the surrounding dirty dishes.

Oh, I'm tired of discussing it. Just get a dishrag!

<u>Dishrags, dishtowels, hand towels</u>

Drape the dishrag over the faucet or hang it somewhere above the sink so it can drip and dry between use. Change it every day.

Hang the dishtowel in a different place than the hand towel. They'll get mixed up once in a while anyway, but that's life. Change them when they apparently need changing or a couple times a week, whichever comes first.

Sanitary Habits in the Bathroom

Bacteria, viruses, and funguses just love dampness. So the best thing you can do is to counteract the damp environment of the bathroom.

Hang towels on large enough racks that they will dry. Reserve a rack for the floor mat, and hang it up after you've dripped on it.

Crack a window open. Ventilation helps things dry and disperses air-borne viruses.

Toilet

Why disinfect the toilet bowl? Germs aren't going to crawl out at night and go looking for you. Besides, I don't think it's even possible to disinfect the bowl. Don't believe me? Read the label on your bottle of disinfectant!

To disinfect something, you have to keep it continuously wet for ten minutes with the disinfectant. How do you keep the near-vertical sides of the toilet bowl wet for that long? The liquid or foaming disinfectant just slides down into the water where it is greatly diluted.

Even the thick stuff like Soft Scrub is not going to fill the bill. For one thing, it's difficult to apply it uniformly without using half of the bottle, and it also slides down after a while. That makes a lot of cleaning manuals rather disingenuous when they advise you to "disinfect the toilet." How? They quickly change the subject.

But what about sanitizing? Did you know there's a difference between disinfecting and sanitizing? I didn't either until recently.

Sanitizing means killing 99.9% of the bacteria targeted by the particular substance you're using. Sanitizing requires thirty to sixty seconds of continuous contact with the sanitizer. That's still a long time, but it's a lot more feasible than the ten minutes required by disinfecting.

Disinfecting kills 99.99% of the targeted bacteria, plus spores. Sanitizing doesn't kill spores. I think that means the spores might eventually re-germify the object. (Sterilizing, by the way, means killing absolutely all microbes.)

A thick coating of Soft Scrub may sanitize the sloping sides of a toilet bowl above the water line. Below the waterline, any disinfecting substance would be greatly diluted and rendered ineffective. So why bother? Scrub the bowl with scouring cleanser and be done with it.

If you're really concerned about germs, sanitize the parts of the toilet you actually touch—the seat and the handle. Also, I think sometimes about the inside of the lid. It must be pretty germy because the flushing action throws microscopic fecal particles ten feet up into the air. If you close the lid first (and I do since reading about this fountain of microscopic shit), it catches them.

On the other hand, public toilets don't even have lids, so how much of a problem can it be? Flush, wash hands, and evacuate.

Hand-washing

Washing your hands after using the toilet is the most effective way of preventing swarms of germs from hijacking your hands and then spreading throughout the house.

However, we're still a long way from foolproof. If you make the mistake of thinking about it too much, the inconsistencies are pretty blatant. For instance, to walk out of the bathroom with confidence that we're not carrying bathroom germs aboard our person, we would need to wash our hands before we pull up our pants. Yes, I know that's ludicrous.

We would also need bathroom fixtures that turn on by themselves—just like the ones in the airport—so we don't re-contaminate our hands by turning off the faucet after we just meticulously cleaned them. Plus we need soap dispensers that we operate with our elbows, and what about that towel? How long has it been hanging there and who used it last?

See what I mean? You can turn into a germaphobe, and it won't do you any good. It will just drive you crazy.

I am going to end this chapter by refusing to give you painstaking instructions on how to wash your hands. Just do it. With any luck you'll nab enough germs that you won't set off any alarm bells when you walk out of the door.

Your own notes

Chapter six

THE BATHROOM

Pretend your mother-in-law is coming to visit

The throne room of King Euphemism may be the smallest room in the house, but it's an important one. We do some of our best reading and brooding in the bathroom. But most importantly, the bathroom is where we ready ourselves to go out into the world. Our homes may be filthy wrecks, but no one would guess by looking at us.

Clean the mirrors first and end with the toilet. Mirrors come first because you want your drying rag to be at its driest. The toilet is last because afterwards you don't want to use that rag anymore. Quarantine it until you can launder a load on the sanitize cycle.

Mirrors

Squirt with vinegar and water, scrub, and use your squeegee. Dry the edges with a dry rag. Or be like everyone else and use Windex and paper towel. Unlike windows, mirrors are pretty easy to clean.

Sink

Get rid of the hair first. Rinse it down the drain. If there's caked soap on the rim, blast it with some vinegar from your spray bottle. Give it a minute while you scour the rest of the sink with scouring powder. By the time you get to the pre-treated area, it should easily come clean. Fill your quart container with water to rinse again. Wipe the rim dry.

Chrome or stainless steel fixtures

If the water spots don't disappear when you rub them with your dry rag, sprinkle baking soda on the main part of the faucet and drape a rag over it. Dribble a little rubbing alcohol on the rag and then saw the rag back and forth like you're shining shoes. Do the same thing between the knobs.

If baking soda doesn't take care of the water spots, break out the steel wool (four zeroes on the package, remember!) Lay the steel wool on top of the faucet (lengthways is more effective than crossways) and drape your rag over it. Pretend like you're shining shoes again.

Now it looks perfect except that there are little flecks of steel wool all over the place! Better rinse and then dry it all over again. You don't want water spots, do you?

Copper fixtures

Just wipe them unless they're tarnished or have funky greenish grunge growing on them. In that case use vinegar and salt. Squirt a thin rag with your vinegar and water bottle, and generously sprinkle salt on it. Then lay or wrap the rag around the aberrant parts that offend you. Squirt again. Let it sit for five minutes before polishing.

Or you can skip the chemistry and just scour them with steel wool.

Tub

Get rid of the hair first. It will only annoy you if you don't. Rinse it down the drain, or you can even vacuum it out

Before you put on your gloves, rub a couple fingers up and down one side to locate the ring of grime. Sprinkle scouring cleanser or baking soda directly onto your scrub rag and apply it to that zone all the way around. When you're through with that, you can finish the sides and bottom of the tub with quick, easy strokes.

To rinse, pour water from one of your quart containers while the other one fills up. It helps to wipe up and down with one gloved hand while pouring with the other.

You may think it's all rinsed after you've tossed a couple quarts of water around, but it's not. Don't believe me? Come back in an hour after it's dry and rub your hand along the surface. See? You might think of that the next time you take a bath in l'essence de Comet. I use at least four quarts.

Caulking

The caulking around a tub and along seams of whatever surrounds the tub can turn a really unappealing shade of moldy black or brown. The only thing that ever works is Soft Scrub, and that doesn't always work if the mold has grown in behind the caulking. Squirt a bead of Soft Scrub along the line of caulking and let it sit for at least fifteen minutes. Sometimes it works.

Tub shower

Remember the 90% rule. A perfectly clean bathroom will make your guests feel bad for using it .

No-slip mat

Flip it over once in a while and see where the black gunk likes to hide. A minute with a scrub brush and a little detergent or baking soda will get rid of most of it. Don't worry about getting all of it.

Soap rack doodads

If you take showers in your bathtub, you probably have one of those little racks for soap and various accoutrements that hang off the nozzle. They're usually made out of coated wire or metal or even wood. They can get pretty gross—usually from the caked soap. Vinegar is the thing you need to loosen up that soap. If it's really caked on, scrape it with a putty knife after you've let the vinegar work on it. Don't worry about getting a hundred per cent—it's just going to get grungy again.

Shower curtain

Has it become so unspeakably gross and slimy that you try not to touch it when getting in and out of the tub? Are blackish dots growing like the plague? You may have to throw it away.

50

But first, try laundering in on a delicate cycle with a couple of big towels or the bathroom mat. To be on the safe side, stop the machine before it goes into the spin cycle or else it might disintegrate. It might disintegrate anyway if it's really cheap or old.

To prevent this sorry situation from developing in the first place, try closing the curtain completely after you've showered. That spreads out the folds and lets air to them. Leave the nearest window open as much as possible. It may also help if you use only one layer instead of having both an inner and an outer layer.

The best idea is to take a pair of scissors to them. Cut off the bottom—leave only enough plastic to overlap the bathtub by a few inches.

<u>Shower enclosure walls—glass, acrylic, fiberglass</u>

Hit them first with vinegar—that will get rid of soap scum and mineral deposits. If the walls are glass, you can scrub them with Bon Ami if they're still cruddy and then rinse really well and use a squeegee. Acrylic and fiberglass walls can probably handle Bon Ami also, but baking soda is safer.

Unglazed Tiles

If the tiles are cruddy, use Bon Ami or baking soda, or squirt a few drops of liquid detergent directly onto your rag and scrub lightly but vigorously. Then rinse with vinegar and water. Swipe with a more-or-less dry rag.

If they're not that dirty, tiles will often clean up with just a squirt of vinegar and water and the swipe with a terry cloth rag.

By the time I read that vinegar is supposed to be bad for tiles,

I had been using it on my clients' tiles for at least five years. Now it's been over ten years, and I still see no problems. I think it's safe to conclude that a 50/50 solution of vinegar and water is not acidic enough to damage tiles.

Or maybe I've been saved by the fact that I always use a final wipe with a more or less dry towel—a move I hope to have impressed on you by now. You don't want a dull, smeared look, do you? Never noticed? Okay, never mind.

Glazed Tiles

Don't use anything abrasive, not even baking soda, unless you test an inconspicuous tile first. Many glazes are too delicate and will develop a faint whitish patch where it was scoured. Liquid detergent and water is the safest route to take.

Tile grout

Many products claim to clean grout. All you have to do is spray it on and then wipe it off. Right. I have yet to discover the product that actually performs that way. I always try vinegar first, but if that doesn't work, then I use a bleach solution or Soft Scrub. (Rinse the vinegar away first because it doesn't mix well with bleach.)

Focusing directly on the grout is the most effective method. Spray or otherwise apply the substance of choice directly on the grout and then use a toothbrush-sized brush. [See chapter 1 under brushes.] It's tedious if you have a large amount to do, so I would recommend alternating sections with doing something else.

Toilet

Throw some scouring powder in there if you haven't already.

When you use the brush inside the bowl, don't forget the bottom side of the rim. (May you never discover what can grow under there.) I also use the brush on the bottom side of the seat.

If your toilet has developed brown streaks—usually a mineral buildup from your water—you probably want to get rid of them before they get too bad. Brown toilet bowls raise unappealing associations for most of us.

First, reduce the amount of water in the toilet bowl. Some toilets will get rid of a lot of their water if you quickly pour a quart of water into the bowl, directly over the hole. If that doesn't work, crawl around until you find the water supply valve behind the toilet and turn it off. Then flush it.

Squirt a line of detergent all around the top of the bowl. As it drips down, use a putty knife to scrape pumice off the stick and onto the sides of the bowl. Go at it with the toilet brush.

If you have to work below the water line, use the pumice stick directly on the problem spot, scraping as lightly as possible. Hope your gloves don't leak.

If the sides of the toilet are ridiculously brown, it would be better to use CLR or one of those products instead of pumice.

Okay, the bowl is clean or clean enough. If you want to pour some disinfectant into it, go ahead. This might be a little more effective than wearing garlic to ward off evil spirits. [See chapter 5 for the full benefit of my sarcasm about disinfectants in the toilet.]

However, you can make a reasonable case for sanitizing the parts of the toilet that you actually touch—the seat, the inside of the lid, and the handle. A coating of Soft Scrub is probably effective—let it alone for three minutes before you wipe it off.

Or those disinfecting wipes work pretty well—especially if you follow the directions. If you apply them amply, the surface should stay wet enough for the thirty seconds it would require for sanitizing. Four minutes actually disinfects, but four minutes is a long time. Use your watch and conduct your own scientific experiment if you don't believe me.

Finish by wiping off the top of the tank and the top of the seat cover and the rim behind where the toilet seat fastens. Lift up the seat and wipe the top of the rim. Now fold the rag over and wipe the part of the toilet that bolts to the floor. Get rid of the rag.

Who needs Drano?

If your sink or tub is stopped up or just slow, you might be able to deal with it, using a piece of wire and some baking soda and vinegar.

Sink drains with built-in stopper

To unhook and remove the stopper, find the metal rod under the sink that sticks out from the pipe. Unscrew the screwy part and pull out the stem that holds the stopper in place.

Now that the stopper is out of the way, use a wire with a little hook on one end (the wires that hold Chinese food cartons together are perfect for this) to fish all the hair out of the slimy depths of the drain. (You'll be amazed and frightened.)

Put it back together and run the water. If it's still slow, take the stopper back out and use baking soda and vinegar ([see instructions next paragraph]. Or just do it anyway. It's fun.

Drains with no built-in stopper

Pull out all the hair you can with your little wire but if the water still drains too slowly, start heating up a teakettle of water on the stove. As it heats drop a couple of heaping teaspoons of baking soda down the drain, followed by an ounce or so of vinegar. Very satisfying bubbling and foaming action will ensue. Repeat the baking soda and then more vinegar several more times until the novelty wears thin. Leave it alone for ten or fifteen minutes before pouring the kettle of boiling water down the drain.

Your own notes

Chapter seven

THE PARLOR AND OTHER DUSTY ROOMS

You don't have to live this way

Are you one of those scarred individuals whose grim-lipped mother made you dust the furniture every Saturday whether it needed it or not? As a professional housekeeper, I have to practice preventative dusting in the homes of my clients, but in my own home I prefer to wait until I can autograph the furniture. Then I break out my array of dusting tools.

The Parlor

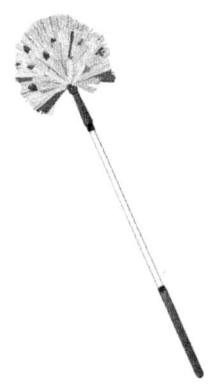

Dusting tools get their bad reputation from people who don't use them properly. Doing it right means two things. First, the duster itself must be clean. Dusting the furniture has a whole other meaning if your duster is full of dust. [See sidebar on pg. 61]

Second is technique. Start with the highest surfaces and work your way down with calm, easy strokes. Ninety to ninety-five per cent of the dust will end up on the floor, where it can be vacuumed or otherwise removed.

You can always go back with a cloth and even a little furniture polish to lavish attention on your most impressive furniture. Furniture polish is best used on a dust-free surface anyway; otherwise it might get grimy.

Overhead dusting first

If it's been a long time since you last cleaned, make sure you look up before you begin. Don't clean the room before dealing with the mess suspended above your head. Cobwebs aren't too bad—you can usually snag those without causing fall-out—but considerable dust can collect on high horizontal surfaces like window sills, ceiling beams, fan blades, picture frames, etc.

An overhead duster is the best tool to use. If you twirl the handle the spinning brush will clean sticky cobwebs out of corners (be sure to check the skylights) better than anything else. If you don't have high horizontal surfaces and the ceiling isn't too high, you can make do with a broom.

If you're in a bedroom, throw an old sheet over the bed, especially the pillows, before you do the overhead thing.

If you dislodge much dust overhead, wait a couple of minutes to let it settle before cleaning below. You can always go to the next room and get the dusting process started in there.

Then the blinds

How dirty are they? Force yourself to examine them. Pinch a blade between thumb and forefinger. Are they simply dusty? Is the dust starting to turn grimy? If you catch them in time, you can use Martha's EZ method—an original method unrecommended by nine out of ten experts.

Are the blinds coated with thick grime? Do they have spots as if something has dripped on them? Poor you! You must do them the hard way.

I have read two cleaning manuals that suggest taking really dirty blinds down and dunking them in the bathtub. That advice goes beyond crazy to downright sadistic. If someone suggests you clean the blinds in the bathtub, nod thoughtfully while backing slowly away. Don't run. It might be dangerous.

Venetian blinds

If they're just dusty--

Open the blinds about halfway. You want a little bit of space between them. With the pull cord in one hand, use a feather duster on the bottom six inches, deliberately whisking back and forth, and then immediately use the cord to pull them up a little. Keep dusting the bottom edge as you gradually pull them up. That's the EZ method. Leave the blinds up until you finish cleaning the entire room. Vacuum your duster.

If they're somewhat grimy—

Close the blinds. Use either the brush attachment of the

vacuum or a dusting brush. [See chapter 1 under Duster.]

Starting at the top, press the blades up against the window while spreading them out a little with one hand. Brush them briskly with the other hand. (Switch hands to brush the side that you were holding.) Do them in sections if they're long, vacuuming the brush in between. Repeat the process on the reverse side if it's in the same condition. Wait a few minutes and then finish off with the EZ method described right above.

If they're really cruddy--

Oh oh. You have to clean each blade with a damp cloth. But before you get started, test a small section to see if cleaning them the hard way will actually accomplish anything. In a sunny location the dust sometimes bakes onto the finish and ruins it. That mottled look might not go away now no matter what you do. Clean a small section according to the following directions and wait a few minutes to let it dry. You can't really tell if it's going to work until it's dry.

If they still look bad, just use the brush and feather duster method. Don't waste your time.

It's better to have several small rags instead of one big unwieldy rag. Saturate one corner of the rag with detergent and water. Windex also works pretty well, and I'm sure some people actually enjoy its mild ammonia fragrance. Starting at

---

Mildewed cloth blinds

Forget everything I said about never taking blinds down to clean them. If your cloth blinds are mildewed, you have to take them down. But don't put them in the bathtub! Put them outside on a table covered with a clean tarp or towel. Spread them out.

Mix a little detergent, a quart of water, and two ounces of bleach. Apply generously with a cloth, or a soft-bristled brush is better. Not a scrub brush. You need soft bristles to avoid tearing up the blinds. (A back scrubber is perfect.) After letting it sit for a few minutes, apply more of the solution and scrub gently.

Hang somewhere dry when you're finished. Make sure they're good and dry before you put them back up.

the top (stand on something so you don't have to work above shoulder level), enclose each blade between folds of the saturated rag, and wipe towards the middle. As each corner of the rag gets black, wet a new corner and continue until you need a new rag. If the blinds are too long to reach in one position, do them in sections.

> Don't forget the 90% rule! No one is paying such close attention to your house that you need to bother with the last 10% of dirt and dust. Anyone who is that observant has no business being your friend.

Music is particularly important for this process, lest you go mad with the tedium.

Repeat: leave the newly cleaned blinds pulled up until you finish dusting everything else in the room

Wide faux-wood blades

This type of blind shows the dust more than the other types, especially if they're on a sunny side of the house. Go ahead and use the EZ method but check them after the room is finished and you've let them down again. You might want to put some finishing touches on them with a slightly damp rag. It goes fairly quickly because the blades are so wide.

Cloth blinds

I vacuum or brush them once in a great while. They don't show the dust much, which is an advantage. However, they mildew easily. See the sidebar for how to deal with that.

The rest of the dusting

Take a feather duster to shelves, furniture, picture frames and the glass, plant leaves, light bulbs, the tops of books, wicker wall hangings, etc., etc., etc.! Hit the insides of window frames and door frames even if you can't see the cobwebs. They're just waiting for you to turn your back.

The Parlor

Make a couple of circuits of the room as you dust everything at a certain level. For instance, do everything with a duster from the top of your reach to shoulder-level and then do everything below that in one or two zones, depending on your furniture.

Keep a dusting brush handy for closet doors with slanted wooden slats or wall radiator slats or furniture with ornate ledges. Anything made out of rough wood—like some window frames or a rustic fireplace mantel--will respond better to the brush than other dusters. Same for bricks, hearth stones, etc. [See dusting brush illustration on pg. 4.]

> ### Dust the dusters
>
> Five seconds with the vacuum's crevice tool is all it takes to clean any dusting tool (and your broom too while you're at it). That includes the lamb's wool duster despite the manufacturer's recommendation to "twirl it outside to release the dust." Yeah, right. Dust does not let go so easily.

Highly cluttered surfaces will need everything removed periodically, and wiped with a cloth, but in between times you can use a feather duster as you shift things around a little.

Electronics

When dusting the keyboard of your computer, turn it upside down. Support one end on the desk or table and use a feather duster or brush. Vacuum the dusting tool first.

Dust LCD screens carefully with a feather duster. If the screen is actually dirty, turn it off, let it cool, and wipe with a fifty/fifty mixture of water and rubbing alcohol. Some experts say not to use tap water, but I've never noticed a problem. Maybe your tap water is more suspect than mine, so it wouldn't hurt to use distilled or filtered water to be on the safe side.

If your computer or other electronic equipment—telephone, answering machine, etc.--is smeared or grimy, use a little rubbing alcohol on a polishing rag. If that doesn't work, use a bit of baking soda, but then you have a gritty residue to deal with.

Rubbing alcohol works well on light switch plates.

Break out the machine.

Vacuum once everything is whisked off. Vacuum couches, heavy-duty drapes, lampshades, window channels and then the floor.

> ### Neat Vacuum Trick
>
> You can clean really narrow spaces—window channels and behind grates, for instance—by enhancing the crevice tool of your vacuum. Take the cardboard tube off of a dry cleaner hanger, cut about five inches off and poke it down into the crevice tool. Your thumb holds it in place while simultaneously sealing the rest of the tool. Cut longer pieces of the tube if needed.

[For pointers about floors— vacuuming and mopping-- see chapter 8.]

Now take one last look at everything. You might use a slightly damp cloth or even some furniture polish here and there for a finishing touch. Flowers? Incense?

Oh. Put the blinds back down. Turn them so they're tilting towards the window. They collect less dust that way.

Miscellany

Animal hair

You can vacuum animal hair off of a couch or chair cushions, but it's faster and more effective to wipe it off with latex gloves. Just put them on and wipe in one direction. The hair will collect in long rolls. This trick works on most fabrics, but not on all.

Mirrors

See mirrors in chapter six.

Really Dusty Books

If there is sufficient room between the top of the books and the shelf above, you can periodically whisk them off with a feather duster. But if there's not enough space, or if you just haven't done them for a long time, a feather duster doesn't cut it. Besides, the pages lengthwise also gather dust eventually, and many shelves don't allow you access to the backs of the books.

Some people would tell you to take all the books out and wipe them onc by one with a cloth. If I tried that I would never finish the job because I'd be reading the books. Leave them on the shelf but pull them towards you and lay them on their spines. The tops are now facing you, and the length of the pages face the top of the shelf.

Now that you have more room and better access brush them off with your dusting brush. Before replacing the books, wipe behind them with a damp cloth.

Water rings on furniture

If you have a faint white circle on a table or arm of a chair, you, or a loutish guest, sat a glass of something on the unprotected wood. No matter how often you wipe it with furniture polish, it remains. What to do?

I've read the craziest voodoo advice about water rings in various cleaning manuals. Some recommend rubbing them, non-stop, for an entire hour with Vaseline or toothpaste mixed with wood ashes. Or you can use cornstarch mixed with your own urine while howling at the moon. Okay, I made that last one up.

I hate to be the one to break the sad news, but short of refinishing, water rings are pretty much impossible to remove. If they bother you, put something on top of them—like a coaster!

<u>Wax</u>

Use a putty knife sheathed with a thin cloth—to scrape off as much of the wax as you can. Then use De-Solv-It to clean up remaining traces.

Your own notes

Chapter eight

WALLS, WINDOWS, AND FLOORS

Must be time to move!

Now we're getting serious! Floors are a routine part of cleaning, but walls and windows always seem like someone else's department. It can take a long time before you acknowledge that no one else is going to do it for you.

Walls (drywall)

Spot-cleaning

Baking soda will scour a lot of stuff off walls, including pencil. New Age Cleaner or Soft Scrub is also pretty effective. Crayon requires De-Solv-It. Squirt it on the rag instead of the wall. If you don't have any De-Solv-It on hand, use baking soda to remove most of it. Or you can have the young artist sign it and then hang an empty picture frame around it.

The whole damn wall

Use New Age Cleaner or some other environmentally friendly detergent mixed with water (1/2 – 1 tsp to a quart of water). Apply generously with a rag or sponge and then use a soft-bristled brush to lightly scrub Wipe dry.

If it smears, squirt with vinegar and water before drying. Dry quickly before it drips and streaks. Actually, the dripping, streaking problem is minimized if you start at the bottom and work your way up.

Prep for painting

In case you're tempted to paint dirty walls instead of cleaning them, let me assure you that that is a bad idea. If you don't wash them first, the paint won't stick. Instead of a detergent, use TSP to clean those walls (found in hardware stores). It leaves less residue than detergents.

Baseboards (really dirty)

Use the same detergent and water mixture (above) or oil soap on baseboards (minimize detergent or soap on unenameled wood). Scrub the top ledge with a toothbrush—I know it sounds anal, but it's your best bet for really dirty baseboards, especially the ones with really narrow tops. Rinse with a vinegar and water squirt and dry with a bulky absorbent rag wrapped around a putty knife. This maneuver will clean that little edge of wall without cramping your fingers.

Windows

Windows are an unforgiving medium in one sense. Almost everything that touches them leaves a mark. Even your attempts to clean them often leave a mark because the light, shining through the glass, shows up every little wet rag stroke you make. You have to keep following through with your strokes until it's absolutely dry. (That's why I recommend using a squeegee.)

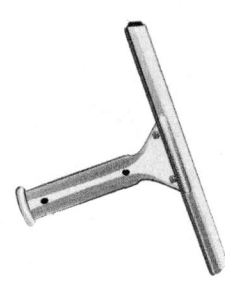

On the other hand it's amazing how dirty a window can get before we even notice it. That's because we're not looking at the window. We're looking at what lies beyond it. Our selective focus rescues us.

But eventually you will notice that window and shudder. Then your view will be compromised until you clean it. For the next few days afterwards, the world you see on the other side will seem brand new.

Use water and a few drops of New Age cleaner or liquid detergent to clean the glass. Oh, all right. You can use Windex if you want to. Scrub the glass clean with a wet rag or sponge. Leave it wet enough to make your squeegee happy.

Run a dry towel along the very top edge of the glass and

along one side. That's the side where you start your squeegee. After each side-to-side stroke, dry the squeegee. When you're finished with the pane, dry any beads of water you see at the edges.

If you don't have a squeegee, get one. In the meantime, wipe the glass dry with your very best lint-free absorbent rag. Finish with an absolutely dry polish rag. [See sidebar about rag fabrics in chapter 1.]

Roll or fold a rug?

FOLD a rug (after vacuuming it) when you're putting it aside in order to clean the floor beneath. Rolling it up will just get it dirty all over again because the bottom of the rug is still dirty. Fold it in half so the clean surface comes into contact with only itself.

Take this opportunity to vacuum or brush off the bottom side. You might be wondering why you should bother to clean the side that doesn't show. (Don't be afraid to ask—it shows you're thinking!) The answer is that walking on crud—even crud on the bottom side of the rug—wears the rug out faster than walking on a clean rug.

ROLL a rug if you're storing it for a few days or more because a long-term fold can damage it. You'll have to vacuum it again once you roll it out, but that's better than lethal creases.

If there's sticky stuff on the pane that won't go away—probably silicone or sap—spray on a little De-Solv-It and then wash the pane thoroughly and squeegee away. If tiny spots persist and you're a perfectionist, carefully use steel wool 0000 [count those zeros!] on them. Rewash if you must.

Floors

Carpets and Rugs

Spot-cleaning--

If you witness the spill, rush to blot up as much as you can with a clean absorbent rag or paper towel, and then refer to the sidebar for specific instructions.

Whether you use detergent or a solvent [refer to sidebar chart on pg. 76], apply it directly to the carpet or rug. Use a rag in a non-circular blotting motion from the outside towards the middle. As long as you can see the stain transferring itself to your rag, keep at it, changing often to a clean part of the rag. When the rag stops showing progress, rinse with a little vinegar and water, then dry the carpet with the same blotting motion and hope for the best.

Who knows? It might work.

What to do if the spot won't come clean:

a) Move a piece of furniture over it. Or a throw rug.

b) Make a whole lot of other spots so it looks like the rug came that way. You can really get into this like Jackson Pollock.

c) Cultivate a spiritual state of acceptance towards the state of ruin that all life tends towards. Reflect on the Buddha's immortal words: "It's already broken." Substitute "stained" for "broken".

Shampooing--

If you have the money, call in the professionals. Believe me, this is a tough recommendation for a do-it-yourselfer like me to make. My experience is limited, but every time I've rented one of those shampooers from the supermarket, it's been an exercise in disappointment.

The machine seems to work at first. The rinse water in the collection chamber looks satisfactorily filthy, yet the carpet doesn't look all that improved once it dries. I've talked with a lot of people who report the same thing.

But there's another problem as well. Even if the carpet does come clean, it gets dirty again unusually fast. This problem seems to be due to a residue of soap in the carpet fibers that attracts and traps dirt. So you're on a cycle that gets shorter and shorter.

If you want to try it yourself, here are two ideas I've run across that make a great deal of sense. One is to use low-foam shampoo (such as Tough Guy Carpet Extraction Cleaner or Redi-Steam) and use less rather than more. A lot of people make the mistake of thinking that more soap means more effective.

The other idea is to put vinegar in the rinse water. You probably think I made this up myself, considering my apparent fondness for vinegar, but I actually found this tip on the Internet. So you know it must be true.

The first problem—disappointing results—might be improved if you had enough time to shampoo the carpet two or even three times. Since the machines are usually available on a twenty-four hour basis, this takes some real organization.

Do all the prep—moving furniture and vacuuming very, very thoroughly--before you go get the machine. Rent the machine around noon. With a little planning and dry weather, you can shampoo in the early afternoon, once again before bedtime, and again the next morning if it still needs it.

The ninety percent rule definitely applies to floors. A pristine floor announces to the world that you never go anywhere or do anything.

Obviously, we're running a risk here of wet, moldy carpets. So go easy on the rinse water and speed up the drying process by opening windows (on a dry day) and using fans.

Non-wooden Floors (tile, faux-tile, linoleum)

Mopping--

I highly recommend using a bucket that is divided into two compartments. The whole idea is to keep your wash water separate from the rinse water. Was I the last person to catch on to this, or do most people still wring filthy used water out of the mop and into the bucket of nice hot water and soap?

When you keep your soapy water separate from the rinse water, it stays much cleaner. The advantage of that is obvious, plus it's possible to use one fourth of amount of soap or cleaner you would normally use.

If you're attached to your regular bucket, you can keep your wash water in a quart-sized plastic container. Splash a little at a time onto the floor. Mop it up and rinse the mop in your bucket of water.

Use a quart of wash water for small to medium-sized floors, plus a gallon of water for rinsing. Larger jobs will require more. I put one to two ounces of Murphy's or Eco-ver or one quarter to a half teaspoon of New Age Cleaner in a quart of water for a good concentrated mixture.

When I talk about rinsing, I mean rinsing the mop, not the floor. I don't think it's possible to effectively rinse the floor. Short of opening a door and using a hose, you are going to end up with some residue of soap on the floor, and I don't see a problem with that.

I don't think I need to tell you how to use a mop, but I have to say there are two basic approaches—faith-based and reality-based. The faith-based approach is one swipe of the mop and then you believe you've done your duty and cleaned the floor. I learned this as a kid and practiced it until fairly recently.

But then I went and became a cleaning professional. Now I actually pay attention to the floor as I mop, pushing the mop back and forth several times over the same area, changing my angle slightly each time in order to persuade dirt to let go of the floor.

Oops. I said I wasn't going to tell you how to use a mop, but then I did.

Here's a good trick: keep a scrub rag underfoot for those tough places that won't come clean. A little leg power is easier and more effective than trying to bring a lot of pressure to bear on the mop itself.

When you're finished you might toss a couple of towels on the floor, stand on them, and slide them around with your feet. Making a network of dry tracks will really speed up the drying process.

Stripping--

If you have some linoleum that is dingy and yellowish and refuses to come clean, you've probably been using one of those squirt-on cleaners with wax built into it. The instructions on the bottle give the impression that a bucket isn't needed for rinsing out the mop. So unless the floor is very small, you will end up with a semi-dirty floor sealed with wax.

I hope you're not in that situation, but if you are, open all the windows and put a clothes pin on your nose because you're going to mix up a quarter cup of Spic n' Span and a cup of ammonia with a half gallon of water. Spread over a small section at a time and let sit for about five minutes before mopping it up. When you're finished, you'll have one clean, if somewhat traumatized, floor.

Wooden Floors

Dusting—

If you feel the floor with your hand after sweeping or vacuuming, you might be surprised at how much grit remains. That stuff gets trampled underfoot as you walk and it wears out the finish. My solution is to use a Swiffer [see chapter 1] after vacuuming—especially on the corridors and areas where people usually walk. It's good for removing animal hair too.

Mopping--

How often should you mop your wood floors?

As seldom as possible is my policy. Wooden floors don't like water, so if they're not really dirty, I would spare them. Spot-clean as much as possible. Drop a damp scrubber rag on top of the dirt and use your foot to work it back and forth.

Scuff marks on polyurethane usually clean up with a little baking soda. But skip the vinegar rinse. The chemical reaction is not good for the finish.

If the floor is a real mess—like a kitchen floor, for instance—go the whole nine yards with a bucket and water and oil soap [see chapter 3 under floor cleaners] and be sure to wring your mop out really well. Most floors these days are polyurethane finishes, which resist water the most, but don't push it.

If your mop is getting old and doesn't wring out that well, dry the floor after you've finished mopping. Toss a couple of largish towels underfoot and scoot around on them.

If your floor is one of those shiny, new laminates that you can practically see your reflection in, you should definitely dry it, or use Bona, the spray-on cleaner. Soap and water will leave little smear marks if you don't dry it.

Bona dries without smearing and leaves a nice shine. Use a Swiffer with terrycloth attached, or one of those micro-fiber-headed tools sold in the cleaning department.

Stairs

Carpeted

Use a vacuum attachment and start from the top, so you don't have to keep lugging the vacuum up from stair to stair. Lugging it down from stair to stair is somewhat easier. If your vacuum hose is long enough, you might be able to leave the machine at the top of the stairs as you work your way down the steps, and then move it to the bottom of the stairs to clean the bottom half. That's as good as it gets.

Hardwood

Stairs often have a worn look right in the middle of the step because traffic is focused right there. Fine grit gets ground into the finish. So after brushing, sweeping, or vacuuming, I often finish off the cleaning process with a big rag. Keep an eye out for spots or patches of crud on the wood. Usually a squirt from your vinegar and water bottle will work well enough, or perhaps a squirt of Bona would do the trick.

Cleaning rug spots

If you know what was spilled, and it's not on this list, try ¼ - ½ of a teaspoon of New Age Cleaner to a cup of water or a teaspoon of another mild detergent. [See general cleaning instructions under Carpets and Rugs; spot-cleaning.]

If you don't know what was spilled, try detergent and water anyway as your first line of attack.

Use vinegar or lemon juice on
rust
mineral deposits
oxidized dirt or detergent (often looks brown or yellow)
old urine

Use ammonia on
fresh urine

Use De-Solv-It (test on inconspicuous corner first) on
chewing gum
crayon
adhesives
grass stains
wax (scrape first)
tar

Use other solvents*
lipstick
makeup
shoe polish
oil-based enamel and paint
ink
felt-tip marker

For fingernail polish, use fingernail polish remover (duh). But then you should probably use detergent and water to clean the polish remover off.

For food coloring and dye, you better call in the professionals, or re-arrange the furniture

*try rubbing alcohol first, then escalate to dry-cleaning fluids like Dryel, Dry Cleaners Secret or Goddard's Dry Clean Spot Remover (found at your local carcinogen store). Or mineral spirits (test, test, test!) might be just the thing for oil-based enamel and paint.

Your own notes

Chapter nine

SPARE YOURSELF

Or save this chapter for when you're old

For the first few years of cleaning houses for a living, I worked like a robot on steroids. I knew certain motions were supposed to do the job, so I did them mechanically and at breakneck speed as if I were trying to set a record. I just wanted to satisfy my clients, collect the check and go home as soon as possible. If I hadn't been approaching fifty when I began my new career I probably would have made it for many years before my body started to complain.

Spare Yourself

I'm going to be uncharacteristically stoic about my list of aches and pains (not enough room). Let's just say they were worth a hundred lectures on body mechanics. I slowed down and started thinking about how to get good results from less exertion. That is when I really learned how to clean.

Somewhat reluctantly, I started paying attention to my motions and to their exact results. I was surprised to discover that deliberate motions were at least as effective as vigorous ones. And I had to admit that cleaning was actually a little more interesting when I adopted a calm, curious attitude.

The following pointers are particularly helpful if you're getting on in years, or you have some physical problems, or you have a lot of cleaning to do. Okay, so you're young and healthy, and you don't have that much cleaning to do. I think it just makes sense to avoid unnecessary strain on your body. Do it the easy way!

So that's my first piece of advice: Choose the easy way. As long as you get good results, do it the easy way. This may be so obvious to you that you wonder why I'm wasting paper on it. I guess I'm slow because it took me years to come to this realization.

My second piece of advice is somewhat similar: Relax! Slow down! The clock on your wall may show that you're saving a few minutes when you rush around like crazy to clean the month-old disaster in the kitchen, but the clock inside your body thinks those few minutes came off your lifespan.

That's weird. Why do I suddenly feel as if most of my audience has evacuated? The only people left have gray in their hair and creaky knees.

Five Rules

Vary your motions.

Don't do the same action for very long at a time. Alternate chores. One way to accomplish this is to clean room by room instead of doing all the vacuuming or mopping or dusting in the house at one time.

Avoid cleaning the bathroom right after the kitchen or vice-versa because both of those rooms require the same kind of scrubbing motion. Do some dusting and vacuuming in between the rooms that require scrubbing.

Alternate hands frequently.
I used to have a bad habit of using my right hand for almost everything. Now I'm fairly ambidextrous.

Use both hands from time to time.
Using both hands is a symmetrical motion that eases the strain. I often use both hands when cleaning counters or walls, and I let my whole torso go with the motion. Try both hands on the mop or the vacuum from time to time.

Use broad flowing movements whenever possible.
Avoid and minimize bracing your muscles or hovering in one position. Holding something up in the air while you clean it with the other hand is an example of bracing that can probably be avoided.

Do not work with your hands above shoulder height.
Stand on a stool, a stepladder, a chair, anything stable!

More Specific Techniques

Scrubbing

Minimize scrubbing! When you have to clean something that is crusty or grimy, strategize and use mechanical aids. The strain of scrubbing can affect not only your entire arm from fingertips to shoulder but also your neck, shoulders, and upper back.

Strategize—

The first line of attack is to soak something if feasible. The most obvious example would be a gunky pan. Fill it with water and soap or baking soda and let it set. Believe me, you'll accomplish more than just putting off an unpleasant task.

Another way of going about it is to apply a wet soapy rag to the problem spot and just leave it there like a poultice.

Mechanical aids—

Scrub brush

But not just any scrub brush. Use the kind with a handle. It's easier on the wrists. A scrub brush is a great tool to use on really crusty dirt and on textured surfaces—something the bristles can really get into.

However, scrub brushes aren't effective on a smooth surface. So I wrap the scrub brush in a rag. It augments the bristles, and you can wet it with whatever cleaner you want to use.

Putty knife

If you're cleaning something narrow—like the top of baseboards—or the edge of a floor or counter where it meets the wall, wrap two or three layers of rag around a putty knife. The blade will focus pressure without cramping your fingers or wrist.

<u>More scrubbing tips</u>

If you have to scrub something hard, try standing on a low stool if the extra height will allow you to work with your arms straightened but not fully extended.

Use your weight instead of tensing your arm muscles. Or instead of standing on something, lower the object by putting it in the sink.

> Need I repeat the 90% rule, or do you have it by now?

Bracing and hovering movements are the hardest for arm muscles, tendons and shoulder and elbow joints. Never hold something up in the air while you scrub it with the other hand. Put the object down before you go at it.

If you're scrubbing or polishing something small, spread the rag out on the counter and use both hands to rotate the object on the rag.

Clean parts of something larger—like the stove grates or pans— right where they are instead of moving them. They're held in place where they already are, so why move them? Well, sometimes you need to soak them. But once you're satisfied that they've soaked long enough, replace them before you finish the cleaning process.

Instead of exerting a lot of pressure on the scrubbing tool or hand, use a brisk but easy back and forth motion and change angles.

Overhead Dusting

Does your neck feel strained if you look up at the ceiling for more than a minute? Wear a cloth neck brace to support your neck when you do the overhead dusting. Make your stick long enough so you can hold it as close to the center of your body as possible. Work at as much of an angle instead of directly above your head. Do one room or area at a time.

Vacuuming

If you're using an upright vacuum, keep your elbows close to your body and walk the vacuum instead of pushing it by extending your arms.

Filling a bucket with water

You don't have to lift the bucket in and out of a sink or bathtub. Leave it on the floor and fill it with your quart containers, filling one while pouring from the other.

Wringing out a rag

If you've ever hurt your hand wringing out a rag, try slowing down. Do it more gradually.

Cleaning the bathtub

Some tubs are extra wide or deep or recessed in such a way that it's difficult to reach the opposite side when you're cleaning. I used go through some real contortions before it finally occurred to me that I didn't have to.

Now I clean and rinse the side farthest away from me while sitting on the brim, with my feet inside the tub. (To avoid taking off your shoes, or getting scouring powder on your feet, use plastic bread bags for protection.) The rest of the tub can be cleaned from the normal crouching position.

See how easy that was?

Your own notes

Chapter ten

TO DUST WE SHALL RETURN

Let's say you've finished cleaning your entire home. It took several hours of your precious weekend—or maybe it took the whole thing! Now you're resting after your labors, congratulating yourself, and doing whatever you do when you're celebrating. But a nagging thought eats a little moth-hole in your victory—it's just going to get dirty again. It's inevitable.

Oh, there are a few measures you can take to slow down the process of deterioration. Getting rid of pointless clutter is a good starter. Anything that just occupies space and gathers dust should have to defend its right to live. But some of that stuff has sentimental value. Like your bottle collection of exotic brews—empty now, of course. Or the shelf full of different turtle figurines—birthday presents from an aunt who's convinced that the turtle is your spiritual totem animal.

One way to reduce household dirt is to take your shoes off at the door. I notice a pretty big difference between the no-shoes houses I clean and the houses where people just trek in and out, dragging a little bit of the outside world in with them each time.

Then there's indoor plants. They not only leak water and drop dead leaves all over the place, the live leaves get dusty. Some people even have trees indoors. Have you ever dusted a tree? I have. It's undignified for both the tree and me. One could argue that trees belong outside with all the other trees.

But you can make the same case for most pets. Shouldn't they be outdoors hunting for their next meal? Dogs and cats are roving factories of hair and dirt. A no-pets household is a cleaner household. But if we keep on in this vein, the children will have to go as well.

In fact, we could just hibernate year round, and that would save considerable fuss and muss.

Some people—not too many--regard housekeeping as a spiritual meditation. They take their shoes off before entering their home as if it's a temple. They wipe out the bathtub after every bath. It doesn't get a chance to get dirty. Mindfully and patiently, they put everything away in its appointed place immediately after using it. This is a fine approach to the challenges of living, but most of us are not ready for canonization. We're waiting until we're old and wise and have more time.

For most of us there is no getting around it. You either got to put aside a certain amount of time every week for cleaning, or you wait until you need an all-day grueling workout to whip things into shape. You either spend the time as you go, or you wait and make one big whopping payment. There are obvious advantages and disadvantages to both approaches, and I'm not here to tell you which to choose.

Whether you intervene often to keep a firm grip, or wait until the Health Department starts threatening you, bear one thing in mind. Your house or your apartment is not a statement of your moral worth. It's not a shrine or a stage or a page in a magazine. It's just a structure with a very practical purpose. The roof sheds rain, and the walls keep in heat and protect you from wild animals.

The cycle of dirt and disorder is an inevitable part of life. From dust to dust we go. So be pragmatic. The housekeeping should suit only the needs of the people living there. You'll work it out, one way or another.

The End

(except for the index)

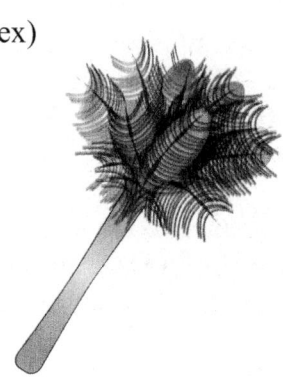

Index

Martha Walden is a free-spirited writer
who cleans house in her spare time. But
seldom her own. Other people pay her to
clean their houses. In her own home she
has a different set of priorities. So she is
both the author of this book and its target
audience.

Printed in Great Britain
by Amazon

11321927R00061